Drawing MONSTERS

A STEP-BY-STEP FUN GUIDE

Published by: **Watermill Press**
Mahwah, New Jersey
ISBN 0-8167-1666-8

Manufactured in the United States of America

BLACK AREAS ARE VERY IMPORTANT IN DRAWING MONSTERS.

WITHOUT BLACK AREAS

WITH BLACK AREAS

DRAWING TIPS

ALWAYS DRAW THE FIRST **2** STEPS LIGHTLY IN PENCIL UNTIL YOU ARE SATISFIED WITH THE WAY IT LOOKS.

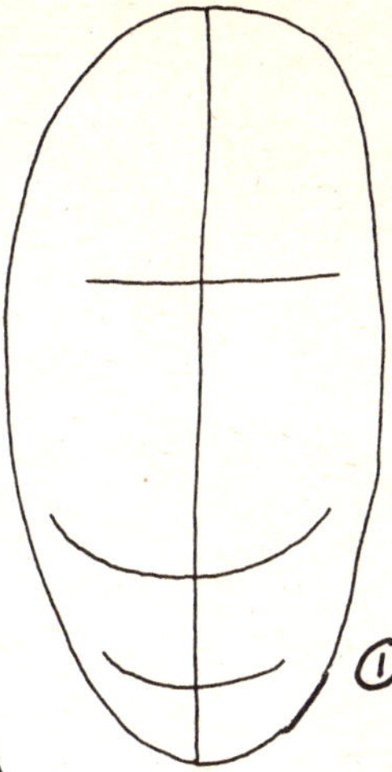

① JUST DRAW BASIC SHAPE

② START TO ADD BASIC DETAILS

HUGO

③ ERASE GUIDE LINES AND FINISH YOUR DRAWING

ADD DETAILS SUCH AS HAIR, WRINKLES, AND BLACK AREAS ONLY AFTER YOU'VE COMPLETED THE FIRST **2** BASIC STEPS.

HAVE FUN!

NIUMES

DRAW THE
FIRST 2 STEPS
LIGHTLY IN PENCIL

A ZIGZAG
LINE GIVES
THE EFFECT
OF HAIR

DRAW YOUR PICTURE HERE

GIGANTOR

DRAW YOUR PICTURE HERE

KLEMPKO

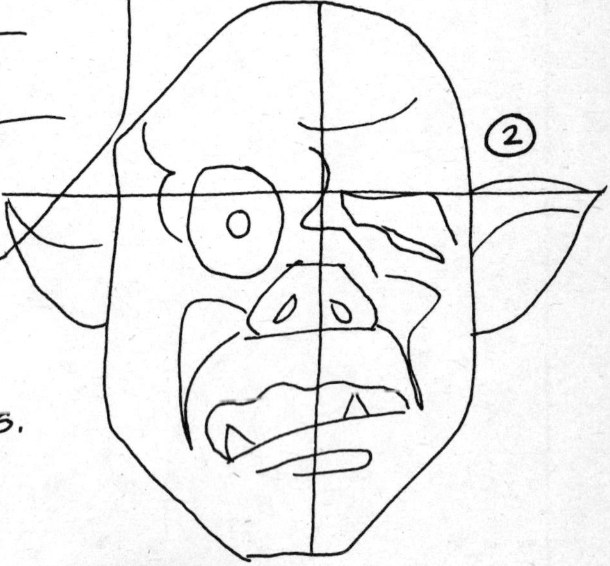

ERASE AS
MUCH AS YOU
HAVE TO DURING
THE DRAWING OF
THE FIRST 2 STEPS.

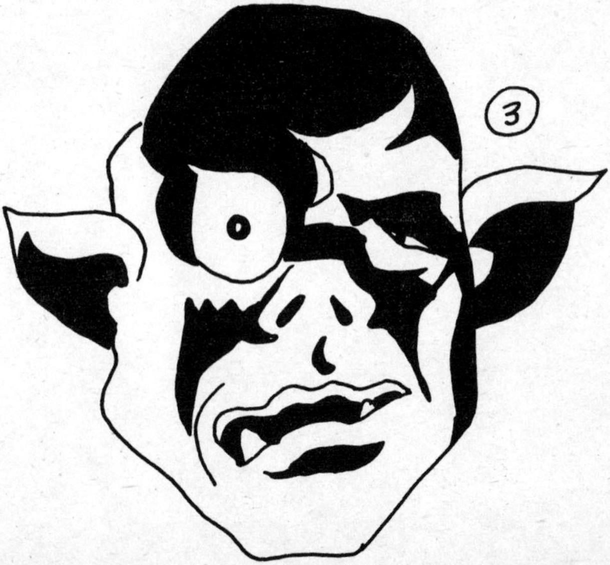

DRAW YOUR PICTURE HERE

GHOUL

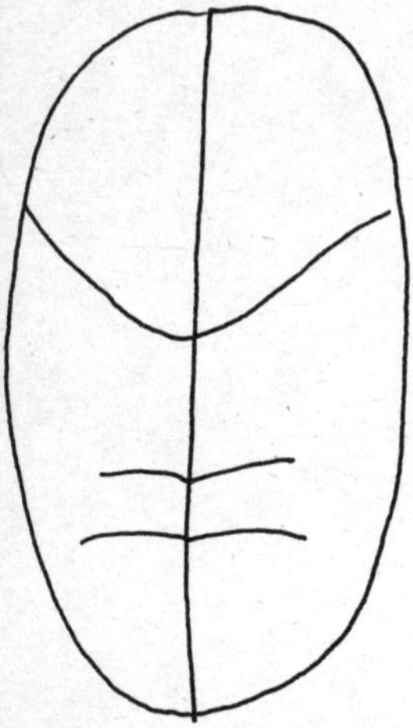

1

2

3

DRAW YOUR PICTURE HERE

DIAVO

DRAW YOUR PICTURE HERE

FRANKY STINE

DRAW YOUR PICTURE HERE

SCREECHER

DRAW YOUR PICTURE HERE

HARG

(1)

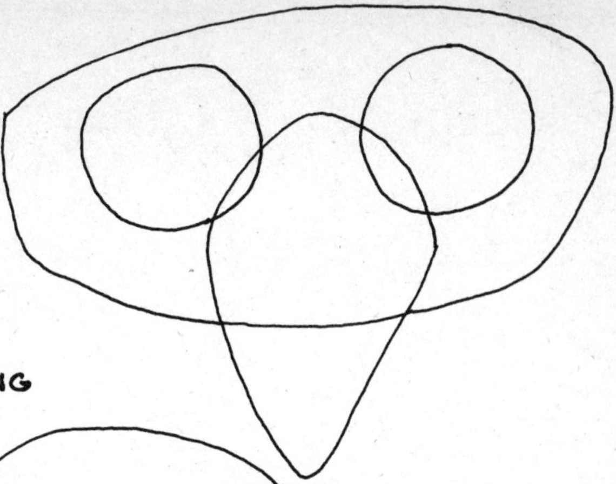

THIS IS NOT AS COMPLICATED AS IT APPEARS. FOLLOW STEPS **1** AND **2** CLOSELY, BEFORE COMPLETING STEP **3**.

(2)

(3)

DRAW YOUR PICTURE HERE

GORGO

DRAW YOUR PICTURE HERE

VAMPIRE

1

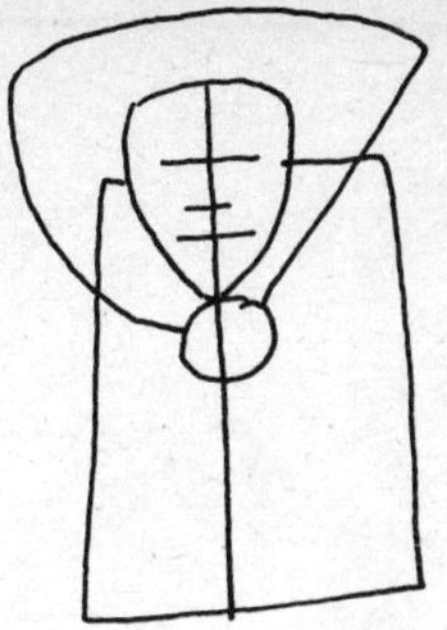

1

2

2

3

3

DRAW SEVERAL FLYING BATS AROUND HIM IN YOUR PICTURE.

DRAW YOUR PICTURE HERE

TAR

DRAW YOUR PICTURE HERE

VEK

DRAW YOUR PICTURE HERE

PUGO

DRAW YOUR PICTURE HERE

VENOM

YOU CAN ADD A GRAVE OR JUST DRAW HER.

DRAW YOUR PICTURE HERE

BRUTUS

DRAW YOUR PICTURE HERE

PLOK

DRAW YOUR PICTURE HERE

MEANUS

DRAW YOUR PICTURE HERE

TRI-HORN

DRAW YOUR PICTURE HERE

GATOR

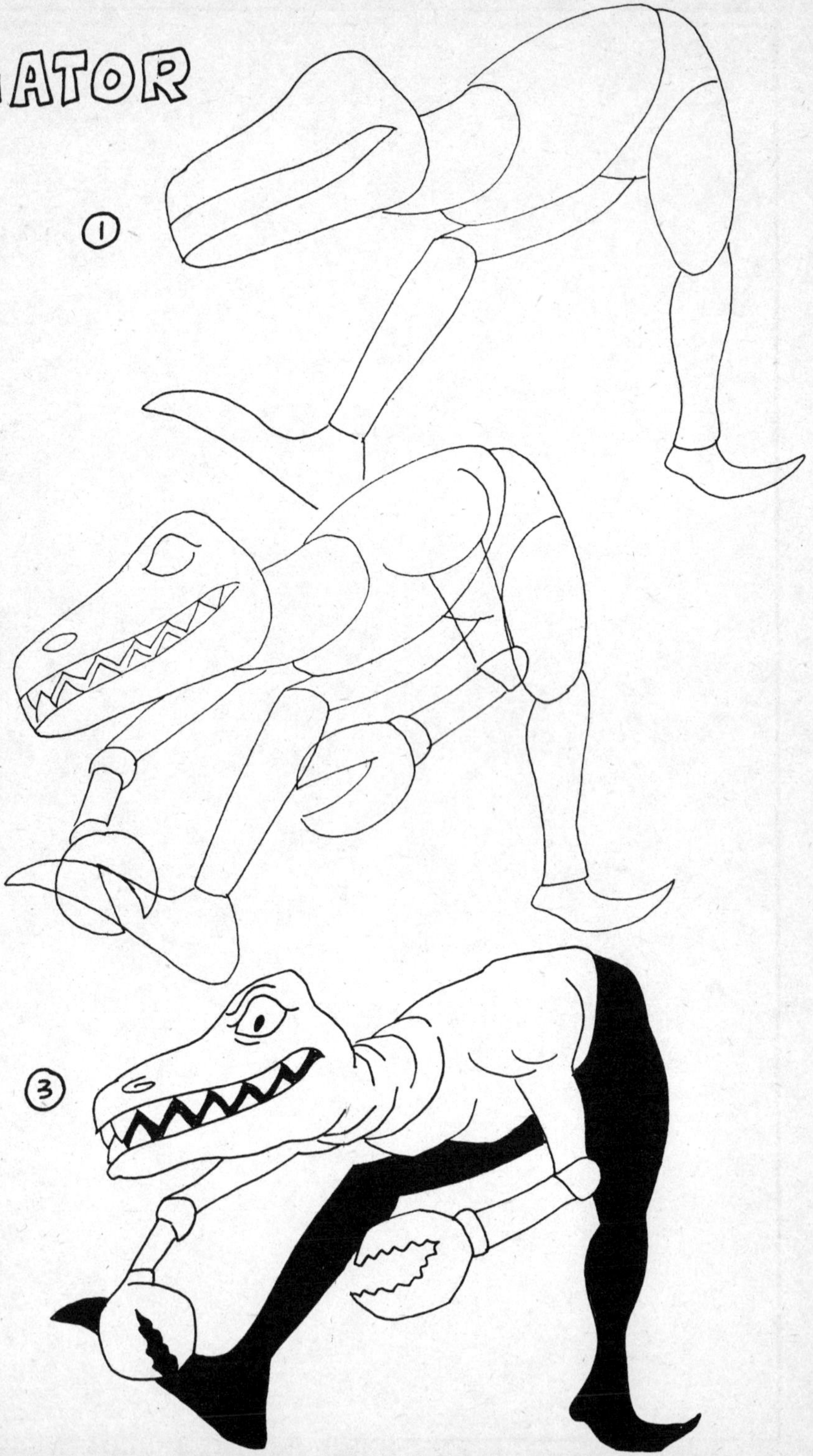

DRAW YOUR PICTURE HERE

MUMMY

1

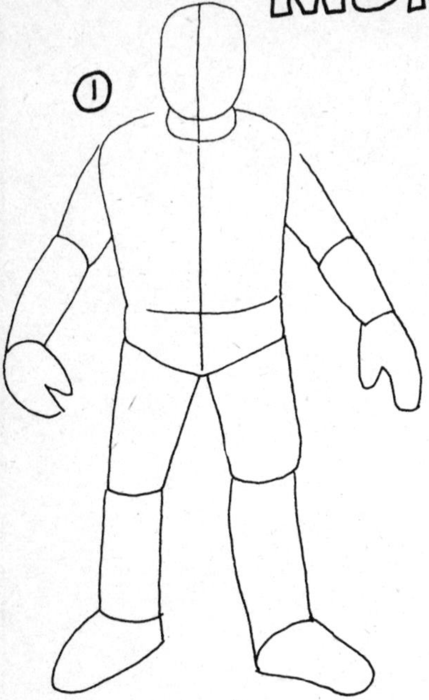

2

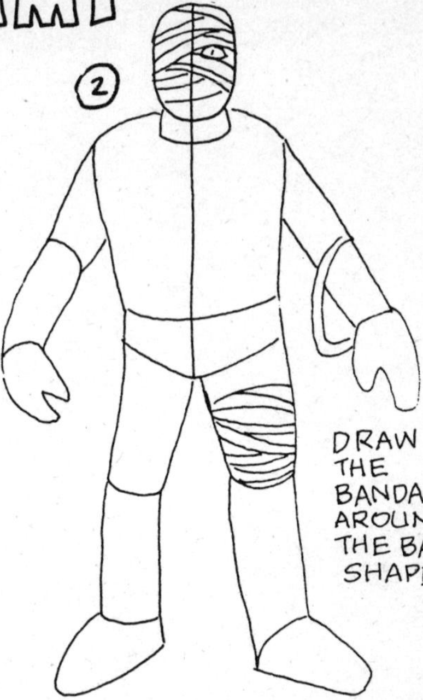

DRAW THE BANDAGES AROUND THE BASIC SHAPES.

3

DRAW YOUR PICTURE HERE

GRING

DRAW YOUR PICTURE HERE

BEAK

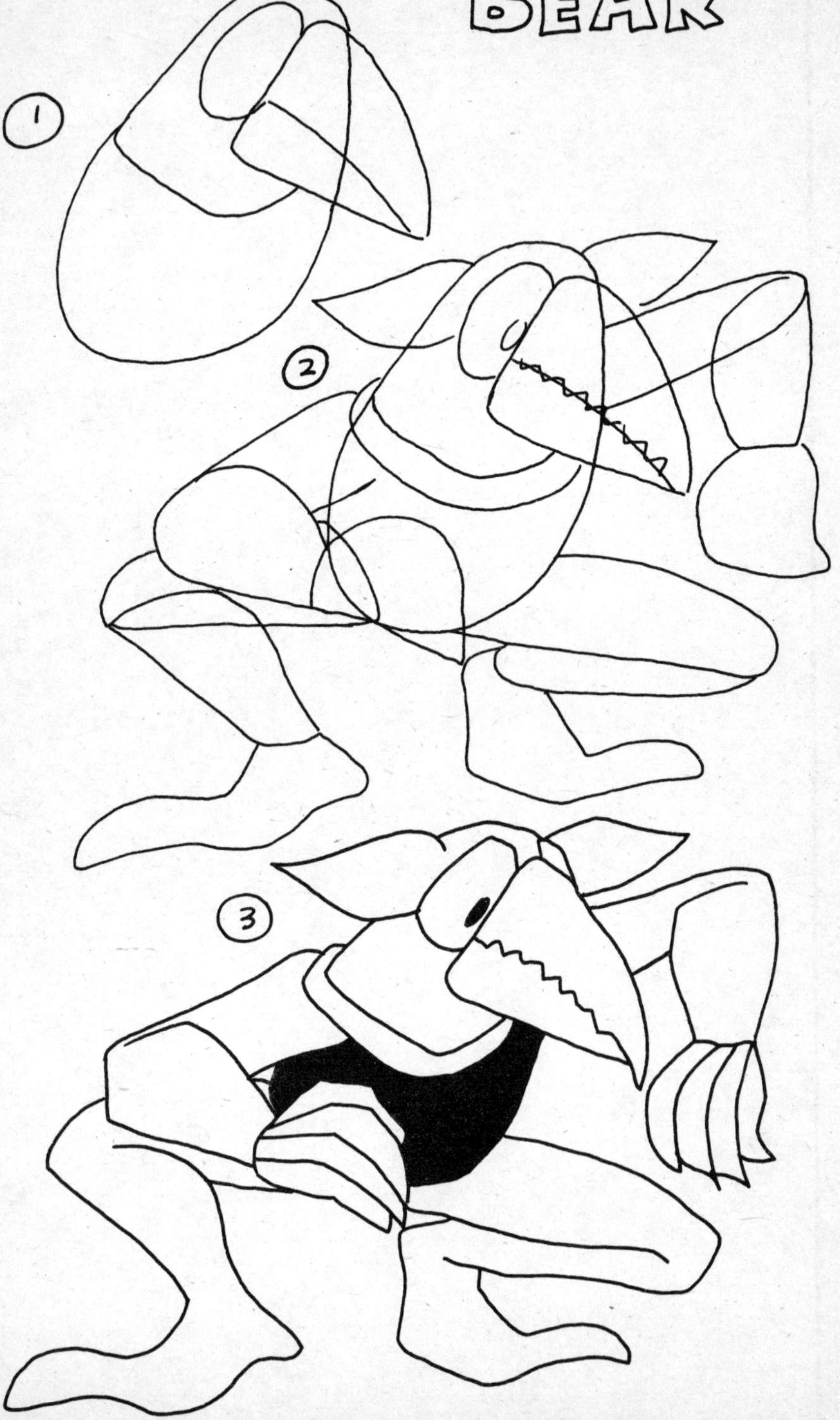

DRAW YOUR PICTURE HERE

MAKE UP YOUR OWN MONSTER DRAWING HERE.